Original title:
Broken Roads

Copyright © 2024 Swan Charm
All rights reserved.

Author: Kene Elistrand
ISBN HARDBACK: 978-9916-89-942-7
ISBN PAPERBACK: 978-9916-89-943-4
ISBN EBOOK: 978-9916-89-944-1

A Sanctuary Among the Scarred Trails

In shadows deep, the whispers call,
A gentle light breaks through the fall.
Upon the path where sorrow tread,
Hope blooms anew, where fear once led.

With every step, the heart finds grace,
In every tear, a soft embrace.
The silent prayers rise high above,
A testament to boundless love.

The scars we bear, like ancient trees,
Stand tall in faith, though bent by breeze.
Their roots entwined, we share the plight,
Together moving towards the light.

In sacred hush, the echoes sing,
Of healing found in everything.
The weary soul shall find its home,
Within the arms of love, we roam.

So walk the trails where shadows play,
Among the scars, we find our way.
For in the sanctuary, we are whole,
Transformed together, heart and soul.

Trails Marked by Tears

In valleys deep where sorrows weep,
Faith's path is worn, through shadows steep.
Each tear a prayer, each breath a sigh,
In the silent night, souls lift up high.

The winding road, with burdens laid,
A whispered hope, where fears do fade.
With every drop, a lesson learned,
Through trails marked by tears, our hearts are turned.

Shadows of the Strayed Shepherd

In twilight's glow, the shepherd roams,
Through silent fields, where lost sheep moans.
His heart aches soft, for those who stray,
Guided by love, he'll find the way.

Yet shadows linger, doubts arise,
In the darkened night, beneath the skies.
But in the stillness, a voice divine,
Calls back the strayed, with love's design.

Broken Altars and Holy Echoes

In sacred places where angels tread,
The broken altars, the tears we've shed.
Holy echoes of prayers long past,
Whisper of hope, a love that lasts.

From ashes rise the dreams once dreamed,
In fallen stones, the light still gleamed.
Each crack a testament, a story told,
Of faith restored, and hearts made bold.

Where Angels Fear to Tread

In darkest realms where shadows dwell,
A light shines forth, a hopeful spell.
Yet angels pause at edges wide,
Where burdens heavy and fears reside.

In every heart, a battle rages,
Life's sacred scroll, with weary pages.
But courage found in whispered prayer,
Breathes life anew, in despair's snare.

Shadows of Grace on Cruel Trails

In the valley where darkness roams,
Faith lights the path, our spirit combs.
Though the journey is steep and fraught,
Love's hand guides, a comforting thought.

Amidst the thorns, blossoms rise,
Promises whispered beneath the skies.
Each step taken in humble prayer,
In shadows of grace, we find our fair.

The mountains may echo our cries,
Yet hope in our hearts never dies.
Through trials fierce, we'll still embrace,
The light that abides, our saving grace.

Beneath the Veil of Asphalt

Beneath the surface, silent dreams lay,
In the concrete jungle, they find their way.
Where asphalt whispers of weary souls,
Each footprint echoes the journey's toll.

Amidst the noise, a gentle sigh,
Hearts yearning for love, to reach the sky.
In every crack, life seeks to bloom,
A testament woven in dusty gloom.

Beneath the veil, hope's light will gleam,
A tapestry crafted from love's pure dream.
In the depths of despair, faith holds tight,
Guiding the lost back toward the light.

Silent Prayers in the Divide

In the silence where shadows align,
We lift our gaze, souls intertwine.
Heart to heart, in the stillness we stand,
Whispers of faith, a delicate band.

Voices unheard, in the space between,
Echoes of love, a serene unseen.
Though the world may tremble, we remain,
Carrying burdens through loss and pain.

In the divide, our spirits take flight,
Guided by hope through the heart of night.
Silent prayers rise, a chorus so sweet,
Binding our souls with every heartbeat.

Whispers of the Spirit in the Wasteland

In the wasteland where dreams seem to fade,
The spirit whispers, a gentle cascade.
Through barren soil and parched dry air,
Life finds a way, though burdens we bear.

With every breeze, a promise unfolds,
In the quiet, a testament bold.
Cracks in the earth reveal hidden grace,
Each step forward, a sacred embrace.

The desert sings in its own distant tone,
In the midst of the struggle, we are not alone.
Whispers of faith twirl on the sand,
Guiding our hearts, a divine hand.

The Pilgrimage of the Forsaken

Through shadowed paths they tread,
In silence, hearts laid bare,
With every step, a whisper,
Of grace beyond compare.

The dust of ages clings,
To weary, worn-out souls,
Searching for redemption,
In lands where mercy strolls.

They gather in the twilight,
Where hope begins to fade,
In sacrifice and longing,
Their prayers yet unswayed.

Beneath the arching heavens,
Each burdened heart will sing,
For in this holy journey,
Their faith shall take to wing.

Alone among the myriad,
They find their sacred ground,
With every tear a tribute,
To love that is profound.

Fractured Footsteps on Holy Ground

Step softly on this earth,
Where angels dare to tread,
For every crack and crevice,
Holds stories of the dead.

The echoes of their voices,
Resound through ancient trees,
A hymn of fractured footsteps,
Carried by the breeze.

In reverence, they wander,
Through gates of twisted stone,
With every prayer repented,
They find they are not alone.

The shards of faith lie scattered,
Among the weeds of strife,
Yet blossoms of forgiveness,
Reveal the grace of life.

As dawn breaks o'er the ruins,
New visions start to rise,
In fractured footsteps, finding,
A pathway to the skies.

Wandering Souls Among Ruined Trails

In twilight's tender glow,
The wandering souls amass,
Among the fallen shadows,
Where echoes of the past.

They tread on ancient stones,
Where faith has carved its name,
Each heart, a flick'ring candle,
In the silence of the flame.

With whispers through the valleys,
And prayers upon the breeze,
These souls, forever searching,
Yearn for eternal peace.

Through ruined trails they venture,
In quest for what is true,
For in the paths of sorrow,
A glimmering hope breaks through.

And as the night encircles,
Their spirits find the light,
Among the shattered journeys,
They rise into the night.

The Crossroads of Faith and Despair

At the crossroads they gather,
With choices hard to face,
Where faith entwines with darkness,
And love becomes disgrace.

In stillness thick with tension,
They weigh each silent plea,
For every turn unchosen,
Leaves echoes of the free.

Yet here amidst the conflict,
A voice calls from within,
Beyond the veil of anguish,
Where hope and grace begin.

In shadows long and weary,
They seek the sacred sign,
To guide them through the tempest,
To realms where hearts align.

For every path of sorrow,
Can lead to love's embrace,
At the crossroads, they discover,
The miracle of grace.

The Fractured Way of the Anointed

In the shadow of thorns, they tread with care,
Bearing the weight of a world laid bare.
Each step whispers of grace divine,
Yet the cracks reveal a sacred sign.

Hearts heavy with burdens, yet eyes so bright,
Guided by stars that pierce the night.
In the fractured path, the light still gleams,
Hope arises, weaving golden dreams.

Cloaked in shadows, the faithful wander,
Searching for solace, their spirits ponder.
With every stumble, a lesson learned,
Strengthened in faith, their hearts still burned.

Through valleys of doubt, their voices rise,
A chorus of mercy that fills the skies.
In the brokenness, they find their way,
For the love of the Anointed shall not sway.

And when the journey meets its end,
They'll stand together, the broken mend.
For in each fracture, a story told,
Of the Anointed's love, forever bold.

Grace Beneath the Stumbling Stone

Amidst the trials, a pathway unfolds,
Beneath the stumbling stone, grace holds.
Each fault bears witness to higher aims,
In whispered prayers, we seek His names.

Like rivers that twist through barren land,
Faith flows softly, a gentle hand.
In our weakness, His strength appears,
Turning our sorrows to hopeful tears.

When shadows lengthen and spirits fall,
There comes a vision, a heavenly call.
For in our failings, we count the cost,
Yet find in His arms, never lost.

Each misstep leads to the heart's embrace,
A dance of redemption, a saving grace.
So let us walk, though paths may wane,
In the depths of our struggle, love shall reign.

At the journey's close, we'll look back and see,
The grace beneath what was meant to be.
With spirits united, in truth we'll stand,
Forever held in His righteous hand.

A Testament to Wounded Paths

In wounds of the traveler, stories reside,
Paths intertwined where sorrow and pride.
Each scar a chapter, each tear a rhyme,
A testament woven through space and time.

Through forests of anguish, the pilgrims roam,
In search of redemption, a place called home.
Every bruise is a testament, bold and bright,
A mark of survival, a beacon of light.

With echoes of faith in the mountain's song,
The weary find courage where they belong.
For the wounded paths are not lost in vain,
But rich with compassion, in love's domain.

Together they gather, the broken and scarred,
Hearts united, though paths have been marred.
In harmony's dance, their spirits soar high,
Like kites on the wind, they touch the sky.

So let every heart, though marked by the fight,
Shine with the glory of hope's pure light.
For in the journey, though fraught with pain,
A testament blooms in the after rain.

The Sins of the Traveler

Through the wanderer's eyes, the world unfolds,
In shadows of choices, the truth beholds.
Each step an echo of paths not taken,
The sins of the traveler, hearts left forsaken.

On a journey of longing, through valleys and peaks,
The silence speaks volumes, the spirit seeks.
In whispers of doubt, the shadows conspire,
Yet grace offers warmth like a hearth's desire.

With stumbles and falls, the lessons emerge,
A tapestry woven, in sorrow we urge.
For every sin marks the sacred embrace,
Of mercy's caress, a holy place.

And as they traverse the landscape of night,
The traveler finds strength in the flickering light.
A compass of faith in the depths of despair,
Transforming each sin into love laid bare.

So let us remember, as we roam this earth,
That every misstep can lead to rebirth.
For the sins of the traveler are steps to the divine,
Each path, a blessing, by design.

From Cinders to Celestial

From ashes bright, a spark does glow,
In darkness deep, the light will flow.
Forgiven souls shall rise in grace,
Transcending pain, they find their place.

Through trials faced, their hearts are pure,
In faith, they stand, forever sure.
With every step, the path unfurls,
To heavens high, their spirit swirls.

Grace forms a bridge from earth to skies,
Where love ignites, and hope complies.
Each tear once shed, a seed that's sown,
In gardens rich, their joy has grown.

Eternal light, the morning song,
From cinders lost, to where they belong.
The journey wrought, a sanctified quest,
In the embrace of love, they find their rest.

So lift your gaze, behold the dawn,
From humble roots, new lives are drawn.
For in this tale, all hearts shall see,
The soaring flight of what can be.

The Parable of the Tattered Map

In folds of time, a journey we find,
A map worn thin, yet spirits bind.
Each line a story, a lesson old,
Of paths untaken, and dreams untold.

With faith as guide, the compass true,
Each step of doubt, a stride anew.
The tattered edges, a sign of grace,
In seeking truth, we find our place.

While mountains loom, and rivers bend,
The heart's desire will lead, transcend.
For every lost turn is a chance to learn,
In shadows cast, see how we yearn.

Through wilderness wild, with courage bloomed,\nIn every trial, the soul is groomed.
With every mark, a promise stays,
The map of life unfolds its ways.

So follow well, through night and day,
The tattered map shall light the way.
Each breath a whisper, each step a prayer,
In this journey sacred, we take our share.

The Covenant Underneath the Cracks

Beneath the surface, where shadows lie,
A covenant forms, it will not die.
In every fissure, a promise made,
Where light seeps in, the darkness fades.

With weary hands, we tend the earth,
In broken places, we find our worth.
The spirits low, yet hearts so bold,
God's love ignites, a fire untold.

For every crack, a breath of grace,
A sacred bond in this holy space.
In unity, we rise anew,
The cracks of life bring hope to view.

In whispered prayers, beneath the weight,
We seek connection, not mere fate.
For in each flaw, divinity speaks,
In silent strength, the spirit seeks.

So cherish well, each broken line,
In every fault, the stars align.
For under cracks, a beauty stays,
In covenant sealed, we find our ways.

The God Who Walks Amongst the Lost

In twilight's hush, a presence near,
The God who walks, with hearts sincere.
In alleys dark, and streets unseen,
He meets the broken, the lost, the keen.

With every sigh, a hand extends,
In whispers soft, the spirit mends.
For every soul that feels alone,
In sacred breath, love is known.

Through storms of doubt, and trials vast,
A light appears, a hope steadfast.
In every shadow, every tear,
The God who walks, forever near.

He weeps with those who've lost their way,
In gentle nudges, He'll not delay.
For in the midst of pain, we find,
A grace that heals, a love defined.

So lift your gaze, embrace His love,
For He walks close, the heavens above.
In every heart that feels the cost,
There walks a God among the lost.

Hallowed Be the Journey

In the light of grace we walk,
With each step, we seek the divine.
Guided by faith, we talk,
To the stars, our souls align.

The path is steep, yet we tread,
With courage held in our hearts.
Though shadows loom overhead,
Our spirit from darkness departs.

In whispers of prayer we find,
The strength to carry us forth.
In unity, our hearts bind,
To the sacred cycles of earth.

With every trial, wisdom grows,
A journey etched in holy ground.
Through struggles, the light still glows,
In the sacred, lost souls are found.

Hallowed be this sacred quest,
For in each step, we're not alone.
In our hearts, love does invest,
And the journey leads us home.

Alms for the Weary Traveler

Oh weary traveler, hear my plea,
In your eyes, the stars have dimmed.
In this moment, let it be,
With open hearts, we will not skim.

Bread of mercy we shall share,
Cup of kindness, filled with grace.
For the burdens, we will bear,
In love's embrace, find a place.

Every step you take with pain,
We will walk beside you still.
In joy and sorrow, we remain,
Together through each winding hill.

Our hands reach out to lift you high,
For your spirit is not alone.
In the shadows, we will try,
To guide you back towards the throne.

Alms for you, dear traveler, take,
In kindness, may your road be cleared.
With every breath, a truth we make,
For love binds us, and hope is steered.

Ascending Beyond the Ruins

In the ruins, we plant our seed,
With faith as strong as ancient stone.
From the ashes, we will lead,
Towards a light that's brightly shown.

Each stone a story, lost yet found,
In the silence, wisdom speaks.
With every heartbeat, we rebound,
Through valleys low and mountain peaks.

Hope rises high like morning sun,
Piercing through the shadows' reign.
In the struggle, we are one,
From past scars, we will abstain.

Let the winds of change blow free,
Reviving spirits long laid down.
As we walk this road with glee,
In unity, wear hope's crown.

Ascending now, we lift our gaze,
Beyond the rubble, towards the sky.
In this journey, we give praise,
For in the heart, new dreams will fly.

Treading on Sacred Soil

With reverence, we tread the ground,
Where ancient prayers still softly lie.
In whispers, the lost can be found,
As the spirits of earth draw nigh.

Each step a promise, a vow we make,
To honor the ones who walked before.
Through time's embrace, we shall not break,
In love's light, we open new doors.

The rustling leaves, a sacred hymn,
Echoing through the trees so tall.
In the quiet, our souls brim,
With gratitude, we answer the call.

Let nature's chorus guide our way,
As we connect with every breath.
In the stillness, we find our play,
Celebrating life, not death.

Treading on this sacred soil,
With every heartbeat, we belong.
Together, let the peace uncoil,
In unity, we all grow strong.

In the Valley of Twisted Paths

In the valley where shadows creep,
We walk a road that makes us weep.
Yet with each step, our hearts do yearn,
For the light of truth, our spirits burn.

The twists and turns may lead us astray,
But faith will guide us along the way.
In trials faced, we find our grace,
And in His love, we find our place.

A whisper calls through the tangled trees,
An echo of hope upon the breeze.
We gather strength from those who roam,
In this valley, we are not alone.

With every stumble, there lies a chance,
To rise again and to advance.
In the depths of dark, we learn to see,
The path of light that sets us free.

So let us walk with humble hearts,
Embracing peace as fear departs.
For in this valley, we are reborn,
With every dawn, a new hope is sworn.

Morning Dew on the Fallen Leaves

The morning sun breaks through the mist,
On fallen leaves, a gentle kiss.
Each drop of dew, a gift of grace,
Whispers of faith in this sacred space.

Nature cradles every sigh,
In silent reverence, we comply.
For in the stillness, hearts awake,
To the beauty in all that we make.

Even in loss, there's life anew,
In every shadow, a promise true.
The fallen leaves, a symbol bold,
Of stories vibrant, yet untold.

As the day unfolds in radiant hues,
Let us embrace the path we choose.
With every step, may we discern,
The lessons life's gentle hands impart.

In the dance of life, we find our way,
With morning dew, we greet the day.
In this symphony of nature's song,
We find our place, where we belong.

Mending Fences, Mending Souls

Fences built from hurt and pain,
Stand between us like falling rain.
Yet hope can mend what's torn apart,
And bring together every heart.

With gentle hands, we weave the threads,
Of kindness shared where silence treads.
For every tear, a smile awaits,
In the embrace of love's warm gates.

As fences fall, walls disappear,
In vulnerability, we draw near.
With open hearts, let us connect,
In perfect peace, we'll resurrect.

Through every trial, we will rise,
Rebuilding dreams beneath the skies.
For in our flaws, we find the gold,
In every story, truth is told.

So let us stand, hand in hand,
In this sacred, united land.
Mending fences, mending souls,
Together, we make each other whole.

The Exodus from the Brokenness

In the desert of despair, we tread,
With heavy hearts and dreams unsaid.
Yet in the silence, hope takes flight,
Guiding us through the endless night.

We gather strength from wounds so deep,
In brokenness, our spirits leap.
For every loss, a lesson learned,
In ashes cold, a fire burned.

Through trials faced, we find our way,
Each step we take becomes our pray.
In the wilderness, we seek the truth,
A journey forged in the hands of youth.

With every dawn, the shadows fade,
In unity, our fears are laid.
For from the pain, a promise grows,
The seeds of love in winds that blow.

So let us rise, from ground to sky,
In this exodus, we will fly.
For in the midst of brokenness,
We find the strength to seek our blessedness.

Pathways of the Forsaken

Through shadows cast by silent cries,
The lost seek light in broken skies.
With whispered prayers that fade to night,
They tread the path, searching for light.

Each step a tale of hope and tears,
In haunted woods, they face their fears.
The weight of hearts, like stones they bear,
Yet faith ignites the chill of air.

In valleys deep, where whispers dwell,
They find a flicker, a sacred well.
With humble grace, they lift their gaze,
Towards the stars, in endless praise.

The echo of the forsaken's call,
Rings out through time, unites us all.
In hallowed ground, they seek a sign,
Their footprints merge with the divine.

Through trials faced, their souls arise,
Transforming pain into the prize.
In unity, they rise above,
With hearts ablaze, they walk in love.

The Pilgrim's Lament

With every step, my burden grows,
A journey fraught with silent woes.
My heart, a map of longing's quest,
In search of peace, a weary rest.

The paths I've wandered, lost and torn,
Through fields of doubt, where hope is worn.
Yet every sorrow, every mile,
Is graced by faith, embraced in style.

Oft have I stumbled, lost my way,
In shadowed nights, I yearn for day.
Yet in the dark, a flicker glows,
A guiding light that gently shows.

In whispered winds, I hear Your name,
A promise born of love's great flame.
With every tear that wets the ground,
I rise again, in You, I'm found.

The song of pilgrims, soft yet strong,
Through trials faced, we all belong.
In unity, we mourn and sing,
Our hearts aflame, forever cling.

Echoes of the Shattered Journey

In echoes deep, the past does sigh,
The shattered spirits drift and fly.
In fragments lost, we find our grace,
A tapestry of every face.

With burdens worn, each heart a stone,
The winds of change, our only drone.
Yet in the dark, remembrance glows,
A sacred bond that never slows.

Through valleys vast, where silence reigns,
The broken souls, in fierce remains.
Yet hope awakens with the dawn,
In shattered journeys, we are drawn.

In every tear, a story weaves,
The strength of those who dare believe.
They rise from ashes, dust, and grime,
To seek the light, to dance in rhyme.

Through trials fierce and endless night,
Their voices call, and we take flight.
With faith renewed, the echoes sing,
In unity, our souls take wing.

Sacred Steps on Cracked Ground

On cracked and broken paths I tread,
With every step, my fears are shed.
In trembling grace, I walk with care,
Each footprint whispers silent prayer.

Beneath the weight of ancient stone,
A journey calls, yet not alone.
With every crack, a story seeped,
Of sacred vows and promises keeped.

The earth may tremble, worn and bare,
Yet hope endures in fragrant air.
In sacred steps, we forge ahead,
With hearts aligned, a path we tread.

In trials faced, our spirits soar,
Transforming wounds to open door.
The cracks embrace the light within,
In sacred dance, we start again.

So let us walk on hallowed ground,
In unity, our hearts are found.
Through sacred steps, we rise and sing,
In every soul, the hope of spring.

The Divine in Divisions

In shadows cast by human strife,
We seek the light, the sacred life.
Divided hearts in search of grace,
Yearn for the warmth of love's embrace.

In every creed, a whisper sings,
Of unity in fractured things.
Each loss a lesson, each tear a prayer,
In understanding, we find repair.

Through mountains high and valleys low,
The path we tread, we learn to grow.
In every clash, a truth revealed,
The holy voice, our hearts be healed.

As rivers merge to oceans vast,
We find the common in the past.
In every soul, a glimpse divine,
A sacred thread through space and time.

Let not division dampen our quest,
For in each trial, we are blessed.
With open hearts, we gather near,
Together, we shall conquer fear.

A Choir of Fractured Souls

From shattered dreams, a melody,
A harmony of tragedy.
Each voice a note, a story told,
In life's embrace, they brave the cold.

The echoes blend, as hearts unite,
In darkest hours, they seek the light.
With trembling hands, they lift their song,
In sacred trust, they all belong.

The winds of change may howl and cry,
Yet still the choir dares to fly.
In every chord, a spirit swells,
A testament that love compels.

With every pitch, the spirit soars,
They gather strength from ancient doors.
A symphony of hope and pain,
Their souls entwined in joy and strain.

In brokenness, their beauty shines,
A testament of love's designs.
Through every shadow, they shall gleam,
In unity, they weave a dream.

Pilgrimage Through the Barrenness

In arid lands where silence reigns,
A journey forged in sacred chains.
With weary feet and hearts aflame,
We seek the lost, we seek the name.

Each step a prayer, each breath a hope,
Through barren paths, we learn to cope.
The starless night, a guiding veil,
The echoes soft, a distant trail.

The sun may scorch, but spirits rise,
In every challenge, no disguise.
With faith as compass, we shall tread,
In every heart, a flame is fed.

The barren ground, a fertile sea,
Of dreams that swell, of destinies.
Through trials faced, the soul takes flight,
In the stillness, we find the light.

With every mile, the vision clears,
In pilgrimage, we shed our fears.
For on this path, though dry and worn,
We find the spring of hope reborn.

In Search of the Celestial Path

Beneath the vault of endless skies,
We yearn to seek the truth that lies.
With open hearts and minds aglow,
We follow whispers, soft and low.

The stars align to show the way,
Guiding souls who long to pray.
Through trials faced and storms endured,
The quest for peace is ever assured.

In twilight's grace, we wander still,
With hope as light, and faith as will.
Each step toward the heaven's gate,
Reminds us of our shared fate.

With every dawn, the promise shines,
That love and kindness intertwines.
The celestial path, a road of gold,
A story of the brave and bold.

Though thorns may prick and shadows loom,
In unity, we burst the gloom.
Together striving, hand in hand,
To find the way to that blessed land.

Healing in the Halfway

In shadows deep, we call for light,
A whispering grace, silencing night.
With every step on fragile ground,
Hope's gentle echo is all around.

Through trials faced, in faith we rise,
With open hearts, we seek the skies.
Each scar a tale of love and plight,
In healing's warmth, our spirits ignite.

Through valleys low, in sorrow's grasp,
We reach for hands, in truth, we clasp.
In every tear, a lesson sown,
From wounds reborn, together grown.

When burdens weigh, and darkness looms,
In prayer's embrace, life always blooms.
The path we tread may twist and turn,
Yet in our hearts, the fire will burn.

So let us stand, united as one,
In every battle, our victories won.
For in this journey, we shall know,
The healing presence forever flows.

The Altar of Lost Connections

In silenced halls, where echoes fade,
We seek the bonds that time has frayed.
With every tear, we light a flame,
On altars built of love's sweet name.

Lost conversations, whispers of old,
In every gesture, stories told.
We gather fragments, grains of dust,
For healing comes from bonds of trust.

In memories held, we find our peace,
From shattered dreams, our hearts release.
With every sigh, a bridge we raise,
To connect the paths of our weary stays.

For every loss, a chance to grow,
In quiet moments, the truth will show.
Through every prayer, we mend and bind,
The altar waits for hearts aligned.

United souls in sacred space,
We seek the love, the warm embrace.
For in each loss, we find the thread,
Of connection's light, where hope is spread.

Serpents on the Twisted Route

On winding paths, the serpents lay,
A test of faith along the way.
With every twist, we find our might,
In darkness met, we seek the light.

Through treacherous turns, our spirits wane,
Yet in the struggle, we break the chain.
With every step on paths unknown,
Courage blooms where love has grown.

The banners waved in storms that rage,
We fight our fears, we turn the page.
For every serpent, a truth shall rise,
In battles fought, the heart complies.

So let us tread with steady grace,
Through twisted routes, we find our place.
In every trial, our faith entwined,
The serpents flee, as love is blind.

In every story, we find our way,
Embracing light, come what may.
For through the storms, our souls unite,
And in the end, we claim our right.

Prayer Among Dust and Pebbles

In dirt and stone, our voices rise,
A simple prayer beneath the skies.
With every grain, a hope we cast,
In moments shared, our spirits fast.

Among the dust, where shadows play,
We search for light, we find our way.
For every pebble, a tale to tell,
In whispered prayers, we dwell so well.

The earth our witness, the sky our guide,
Through humble paths, we bide our pride.
In unity, our silence speaks,
The heart of God in every peak.

So let us gather, hand in hand,
Among the dust, together stand.
For in the pebbles, treasures lie,
In every prayer, we touch the sky.

And when the night draws close and near,
Among the stones, we shed our fear.
In sacred space, we find our grace,
In prayerful whispers, love embraces.

Remnants of a Lost Faith

In shadows deep, the whispers call,
Forgotten echoes, rise and fall.
Once vibrant hearts, now filled with woe,
In silent prayers, we seek to know.

The altar crumbles, dimmed by time,
The fading light, a sorrowed chime.
Yet in the dusk, a flicker stirs,
A hope reborn as spirit purrs.

Each tear a testament to grace,
In longing hearts, we dare to face.
Through broken dreams, we wander still,
Embracing faith, we seek His will.

The remnants whisper tales of old,
Of love and mercy, brave and bold.
In every loss, we find renewed,
A sacred joy, by grief imbued.

So gather close, ye weary souls,
In unity, our path unfolds.
With every beat, our hearts align,
In remnants lost, His will divine.

The Crossroads of Despair

At twilight's edge, where shadows blend,
A weary soul begins to bend.
Two paths before, both rough and steep,
In silence, thoughts disturb my sleep.

The weight of doubt, a heavy chain,
In solitude, I bear the pain.
Yet glimmers break through darkened skies,
A whispering hope that never dies.

Choose wisely here, the spirits say,
For faith can light the darkest way.
In fervent prayer, I seek the sign,
With trembling hands, to You, I pine.

Oh guide me, Lord, through this dark night,
To trust in love, to find the light.
With every tear that falls in prayer,
A promise blooms, beyond despair.

For though the road may twist and turn,
In every trial, my spirit learns.
With courage found, I'll face the dawn,
In faith renewed, I shall move on.

Halos in the Dust

Among the ruins where lost dreams lie,
A sacred whisper fills the sky.
With every breath, a story weaves,
Of hope reborn, my heart believes.

In scattered pieces of shattered grace,
I seek Your light, I long to trace.
The dust may cloak what once was pure,
Yet through the haze, Your love is sure.

In every heart, a halo shines,
The remnants hold, the truth defines.
Though life may bruise and wound the soul,
In dust, I find I can be whole.

Through trials faced, I rise anew,
In deepest pain, Your warmth shines through.
With every fall, I learn to trust,
With faith that holds, our dreams combust.

So let the dust surround my feet,
For in the ashes lies the sweet.
A testament to love's great scope,
In halos bright, I find my hope.

Wanderer's Prayer Amidst Ruins

Oh guide my steps, in lands unknown,
A wanderer's prayer, in silence sown.
Through ancient paths, I seek Your face,
In mystic realms, I long for grace.

The echoes whisper, the winds they moan,
In every fragment, a heart of stone.
Yet in my chest, a fire ignites,
Your love, my beacon, through darkest nights.

Amidst the ruins, I pause and kneel,
In gentle whispers, Your truth reveal.
With every breath, my spirit soars,
In barren lands, my soul restores.

Let not despair consume my mind,
In weary hearts, Your peace I'll find.
For every step, I walk with You,
A wanderer's journey made anew.

So bless my path, where few may tread,
In every tear, with love I'm fed.
In ruins deep, my soul shall rise,
Through faith unbroken, I claim the skies.

Sanctified Detours

In the quiet of morn, I kneel,
Seeking wisdom that the heart can feel.
Paths may twist in the light divine,
Each step guided by a plan benign.

Mountains high, valleys low,
In faith's embrace, I learn to grow.
The road is winding, but not in vain,
Every struggle will yield a gain.

Whispers of love in the softest breeze,
Remind me always to bend my knees.
With every stumble, I rise again,
Trusting the path beyond the pain.

Blessed detours, lessons learned,
In trials' fire, my spirit burned.
With every falter, grace does shine,
In sacred moments, I call Him mine.

So lead me on, through shadow and light,
In every step, find strength to fight.
For with each turn, I sing His song,
In His embrace, where I belong.

Lost in the Wilderness of Broken Dreams

In the desert vast, my heart does roam,
Searching for solace, longing for home.
Mirages shimmer, haunting the night,
Yet in my spirit, shines a flickering light.

Tears like rain in the parched earth fall,
Amidst the silence, I hear Your call.
With broken dreams scattered like dust,
I cling to hope, in You I trust.

Wilderness whispers, echoes of pain,
Yet all is not lost, for joy remains.
Each step through thorns, a glimpse of grace,
In every shadow, I seek Your face.

Through trials deep, my soul may yearn,
But in surrender, Your love I learn.
Beyond the desert, lies a promise new,
A garden blooming, nurtured by You.

So guide me, Lord, through the arid land,
Take my brokenness, hold my hand.
In the wilderness, I rise and dream,
Transformed by love, light's gentle beam.

Paved with Ashes and Grace

In the ruins where hope may seem lost,
Each ember whispers, counting the cost.
From ashes, a beauty begins to rise,
Grace unseen, like stars in the skies.

For every ending bends to a start,
Renewal blooms within a shattered heart.
With faith as the flame, I'll find my way,
Through the darkest night into dawn's first ray.

Past sorrows linger like shadows cast,
Yet love's gentle touch frees me from the past.
A tapestry woven with threads of strife,
In the fabric of pain, a glimpse of life.

Let not the ashes define who I am,
In trials' fire, I learn to stand.
A phoenix rises, wings spread wide,
With every breath, You're by my side.

So I walk this path, with courage ablaze,
Paved with ashes and woven with grace.
In every moment, I cherish the space,
Where love redeems and meets me in place.

Straying into Sacred Shadows

Amidst the shadows, where silence holds,
Lies the sacred, the story unfolds.
In moments wandering, lost yet found,
I hear the whisper of love profound.

Straying from light, my heart feels the weight,
Yet grace surrounds me, a divine embrace.
In the twilight where shadows blend,
I learn the truth that love won't end.

Each step I take, Your presence near,
Guiding my spirit, calming my fear.
Through valleys deep, and mountains high,
In every shadow, You are nigh.

With open arms, You welcome me in,
In straying steps, I find my kin.
Through the darkness, stars will ignite,
A beacon of hope, breaking the night.

So in the twilight, my heart will sing,
For every shadow reveals Your wing.
In sacred spaces, I draw my breath,
In straying moments, I find Your depth.

The Silent Witness of Cracked Pavements

In shadows cast by ancient stones,
A whisper speaks where silence moans.
Each crack a tale, a soul's lament,
Bearing witness to lives well spent.

Beneath the weight of time's embrace,
The pavement holds a sacred space.
With every step, a prayer unfolds,
In worn-out paths, His story molds.

The echoes of the lost reside,
In fissures deep, where hopes collide.
Yet in the broken, light shall flow,
From shattered dreams, His love will show.

Faith walks softly on this ground,
Where silent cries of peace abound.
The cracked pavements, a guide through strife,
Remind us of the heart's true life.

And as we tread on weary ways,
We find the Lord in shadowed bays.
In brokenness, He lifts our gaze,
His grace restored through all our days.

Glimmers of Grace on Winding Trails

On winding trails where footsteps tread,
Glimmers of grace, where angels led.
Through twisted paths, the faithful roam,
In each soft breeze, they find their home.

The sun breaks forth, a gentle kiss,
Illuminating every bliss.
With every turn, a lesson learned,
In nature's book, our hearts discerned.

Among the thorns, the blossoms thrive,
In struggles fierce, we feel alive.
His presence lingers in the air,
In winding trails, we find His care.

The journey calls, a sacred quest,
Where weary souls find peace and rest.
With hope renewed, we walk with grace,
Each winding trail, a holy space.

In every bend, His love appears,
Transforming sorrows into cheers.
Through glimmers bright, our eyes will see,
The winding trails that set us free.

Torn Paths of Redemption

On torn paths where shadows dwell,
Echoes of grace begin to swell.
Each step a prayer with hope reborn,
In fractured earth, our spirits mourn.

Yet mingled in that pain we find,
A promise sweet, His truth enshrined.
For every tear that marks the ground,
In deepened roots, redemption's found.

The broken ways, a canvas bare,
Where hearts are mended, freed from despair.
Amidst the ruins, love will rise,
Transforming sorrow into skies.

For torn paths lead us to the light,
Through trials faced, we gain new sight.
In darkness dense, a beacon glows,
With every hardship, His love grows.

So let us walk this path of grace,
Embrace the scars, this holy place.
For in redemption's gentle clasp,
We find the strength in love's warm grasp.

The Journey through Shattered Highways

Through shattered highways, souls we trace,
In broken dreams, we find our place.
With every mile, a story told,
Of faith that walks in courage bold.

In every crack, a promise glows,
A journey marked with highs and lows.
Though rough the road, we hold His hand,
And trust that He will help us stand.

Each turn reveals a lesson dear,
In whispers soft, He draws us near.
Through trials vast, our spirits soar,
In shattered pathways, we are restored.

For every stumble, grace will rise,
Transforming tears to joyful cries.
With hearts aligned to heaven's call,
We rise again, united all.

So let us walk this journey true,
With shattered highways guiding through.
In every scar, His love shall gleam,
And in the chaos, we will dream.

The Ghosts of Yesterday's Footprints

In the silence of the night, they tread,
Echoes of prayers quietly said.
Shadows dance along the way,
Guiding souls that have lost their way.

Whispers of faith in the gentle breeze,
Carrying hope like autumn leaves.
Each step a story, a lesson learned,
In the heart of the seeker, a flame always burned.

Footprints etched in the sands of time,
Resounding truths in rhythm and rhyme.
With every stumble, the spirit grows,
Beneath the gaze of the heavens' glow.

They walk with grace, they walk with light,
Bearing burdens through the endless night.
Anointing the weary with love's embrace,
In the tapestry of life, they find their place.

Embrace the ghosts, let them guide,
In every sorrow, in every tide.
For yesterday whispers, today is new,
In the dance of epochs, we find what is true.

Lessons from a Worn-Out Journey

Along the path where worries fade,
Each wrinkle a memory, each scar a blade.
In the tapestry woven with trials faced,
Resilience shines, in grace embraced.

The valleys echo with prayers once lost,
Where faith was tested and hearts embossed.
Every stone beneath our feet,
Holds wisdom ancient, bittersweet.

We gather knowledge like fallen rain,
Quenching thirst from sorrow's pain.
Through worn-out shoes, our spirits soar,
In pilgrimage, we find the door.

In every stumble, in every tear,
A lesson echoes for those who hear.
Paths of thorns and paths of light,
Lead us towards the divine insight.

Embrace the journey, let it unfold,
For in weary days, life's truths are told.
With every heartbeat, we learn to see,
The beauty born from humility.

Beneath the Weight of the World

When the heaviness wraps like a shroud,
And the silence is louder than a crowd,
Lift your eyes to the heavens above,
Seek the strength that comes from love.

In the depths of despair, find light's embrace,
For even in darkness, there's a sacred place.
With whispered prayers, we rise anew,
Trusting in faith to guide us through.

Each burden carried on tired backs,
Turns into wisdom in life's cruel tracks.
Beneath the weight, the spirit grows,
In the cracks of sorrow, beauty flows.

Let the world weigh as it may,
With every breath, we find our way.
In the storm's chaos, serenity reigns,
In trials, the heart forever gains.

So stand tall, though the night is long,
For the weary wanderer is always strong.
In unity of spirit, we are not alone,
Together, beneath the weight, we've grown.

Seraphim in the Silt

In the stillness of a quiet dawn,
Faithful spirits gaze upon.
Amid the mire and earthly toil,
Angels walk 'neath heaven's soil.

Through shadows thick and laughter wide,
Find sacred grace in the heart's divide.
For where the dirt and blessings meet,
A testament of love is complete.

With every heartbeat, the humble rise,
Seraphim spread their radiant skies.
In the silt of life's intricate dance,
We discover hope in chance after chance.

Each tear like rain, each joy like sun,
In the fabric of time, all are one.
Through earthly struggles, we learn to see,
In the silted ground, our souls fly free.

So treasure the moments, both bitter and sweet,
For every encounter is a divine greet.
Beneath the burden, angels sing,
In the quiet earth, new life will spring.

Echoes of a Fragmented Journey

In shadows deep, a voice I hear,
Whispers of hope, dispelling fear.
Every step, a lesson learned,
In trials faced, the spirit yearned.

Fragments gathered, time unites,
In the silence, sacred rites.
Guided by a gentle hand,
I walk anew on holy land.

Through valleys low, to mountains high,
I seek the truth beneath the sky.
With faith as light, I forge ahead,
For every tear, a path is spread.

In every wound, the grace revealed,
A broken heart, yet love concealed.
Echoes of a journey bright,
In darkness blooms the sacred light.

The path may twist, the road may bend,
But I believe, beyond the end.
In shattered dreams, a message clear,
Embrace the pain, hold it near.

Remnants of Divinity in Mended Paths

A lantern flickers in the night,
Guiding souls to seek the light.
In brokenness, we find our way,
Each heart a star, in night's array.

Mended paths of grace we walk,
In whispered prayers, our spirits talk.
Echoes linger in the still,
With every step, we bend our will.

Once lost, now found, we rise again,
In shared warmth, we conquer pain.
The beauty lies in scars we bear,
A testament of love and care.

Remnants of divinity shine bright,
In unity, we chase the light.
Through trials faced, we understand,
Together we heal, hand in hand.

In every tear, the life unfolds,
A tapestry of stories told.
With faith restored, we shall believe,
In mended paths, we shall achieve.

The Broken Compass of the Heart

A compass shattered, yet still it spins,
Mapping the depth of our internal sins.
With every heartbeat, a choice is made,
In shadow and light, our fears displayed.

Navigating through stormy seas,
The heart learns truth in gentle pleas.
Though guidance falters, love leads the way,
In brokenness, we find our play.

When doubt arises and faith grows thin,
I seek the spark buried within.
A beacon kindles through night's despair,
In every stumble, we find a prayer.

The compass spins, yet still I trust,
For in the journey lies the just.
Through winding roads, I find my peace,
In love's embrace, my fears release.

A heart once lost, now seeks the stars,
Guided by hope that heals the scars.
No longer broken, I rise anew,
With every pulse, to Love I'll be true.

Revelations on the Winding Way

On winding paths where shadows play,
Revelations come to light the way.
Each twist and turn, a secret told,
In faith we find, through hearts so bold.

The silence speaks in sacred tones,
A symphony of spirit's drones.
In every pause, a deeper grace,
In every moment, love's embrace.

The journey long, yet never vain,
In trials faced, we glean the gain.
With open hearts, we walk the line,
In unity, our souls entwine.

The winding way may sometimes lead,
To valleys low, or hearts that bleed.
Yet in the struggle, strength is found,
In every loss, a love unbound.

Revelations shining through the strife,
Remind us of our sacred life.
With every step, the truth will rise,
Guided by love that never lies.

The Halo in the Dust

In shadows deep, where hope feels lost,
A gentle light appears, no matter the cost.
It dances soft through twilight's grace,
A halo shines, a warm embrace.

The weary heart finds peace anew,
In every grain, the sacred view.
With whispers sweet, the spirit sings,
Reviving joy that faith back brings.

From ashes rise the dreams once bold,
In every fold, a story told.
Through trials bare, and weary plight,
The halo glows with purest light.

So lift your gaze, let burdens fade,
In every moment, love's cascade.
The dust will clear, the path will show,
The grace abounds, and spirits grow.

In unity, we walk as one,
With whispering winds, the journey's begun.
The halo in the dust, we find,
A testament to the divine.

Reclamation of the Fallen Road

Upon the path that time forgot,
With stones that bear the weight of thought.
We tread through lost and weary sighs,
To find redemption in the skies.

Each step we take, a prayer we weave,
In silent hope, we dare believe.
Through thorny brush, our hearts arise,
Embracing light, our spirits wise.

The fallen road brings lessons deep,
Awakening dreams from endless sleep.
With open eyes, we see the truth,
In every struggle, there's pure youth.

Reclaimed by faith, we walk with grace,
As shadows flee from love's embrace.
With every tear and joyful sound,
The fallen road, our strength is found.

So let us join in steady stride,
With courage strong, and hearts untied.
A journey blessed, no longer lost,
Reclaiming joy, despite the cost.

The Lost Shepherd's Way

In valleys low, where silence weeps,
The shepherd calls, the wanderer keeps.
Through fields of doubt, his voice resounds,
In every heart, salvation found.

The way may twist, the path unclear,
Yet love abides, and holds us near.
With fervent hope, we chase the light,
The lost will find their way tonight.

From shadows thick, to meadows wide,
Each step a pledge, we will not hide.
With gentle hands, he leads the weak,
In every loss, the truth we seek.

So let us gather, lost no more,
In unity, we shall restore.
The shepherd's way, a guiding star,
With love, we rise, no matter how far.

In every heart, a flame ignites,
Through love's embrace, we claim our rights.
The lost shall find their chosen place,
In every smile, the shepherd's grace.

Between Heaven and the Fallen Earth

In twilight's glow, where worlds collide,
We stand between, with arms open wide.
A bridge of prayer connects the two,
Between heaven's grace and earth's deep blue.

With aching hearts, we seek the light,
To banish darkness, to set wrongs right.
In whispered hopes, our spirits soar,
The sacred bond becomes much more.

The path we walk is often steep,
Yet faith will guide us through the deep.
With every step, the heavens call,
Embracing love that conquers all.

Between the realms, the truth will flow,
In every heart, the seeds we'll sow.
In unity, our voices raise,
To hymn the world with endless praise.

So let us tread with gentle grace,
For every soul deserves a place.
Between heaven's might and earth's own worth,
We find the love that gave us birth.

The Curse of Untraveled Roads

In shadows deep the traveler treads,
Abandoning grace where the silence spreads.
Eager feet upon the cursed ground,
Whispers of hope in the darkness found.

The journey long leads hearts astray,
With every step, the light decays.
Through winding paths of doubt and fear,
The soul seeks solace, a whisper near.

Worn maps forgotten in the dust,
Beneath the stars, they yearn and trust.
Yet curses linger on the breeze,
As prayers ascend like rustling leaves.

In the midst of night, the stars align,
A faint glow shines, a sacred sign.
Hold fast the flame, let it not fade,
For untraveled roads bring wisdom made.

Awake the spirit from its tomb,
Embrace the dawn, dispel the gloom.
With every stride, the heart shall grow,
And banish the curse of roads unknown.

Chasing Light on Darkened Paths

Upon the road where shadows weave,
A soul embarks, unwilling to grieve.
With every step, a flicker bright,
Chasing the echoes of fading light.

The nightingale sings a haunting tune,
Beneath the watch of the pale moon.
In every corner, darkness tries,
Yet hope ignites, and fear defies.

With fervent hearts that yearn to soar,
They seek the dawn, forevermore.
Though tempests rise, and storms be near,
The path of light draws ever clear.

In twilight's grip, the spirit seeks,
Illuminated truths in whispers speaks.
Enduring trials, they stand as one,
Chasing the light until the day is done.

No matter how the night may fall,
The promise of dawn is a sacred call.
For in the dark, there's strength to find,
In chasing light, the spirit's blind.

The Spirit's Quest through Desolation

In barren lands where spirits roam,
A quest unfolds, a path to home.
With every sigh, the echoes flow,
Through desolation, the heart must grow.

The sands of time beneath them shift,
In search of grace, a mighty gift.
Yet courage blooms amidst the strife,
An ember burns, the spark of life.

Spirits whisper on the wind's embrace,
Guiding the seeker toward a place.
Where broken dreams lie on the ground,
Yet in their shards, new hope is found.

Through deserts vast, the heart will race,
A pilgrimage of sacred grace.
Resilience forged in trial's fire,
Reclaims the path that dreams inspire.

In desolation, beauty hides,
An invitation where faith abides.
For every spot the spirit fest,
Is part of love, the great quest blessed.

Praise Songs for the Lost Wanderer

O sing the praise of souls untamed,
In wanderlust, they find no shame.
Through valleys low and mountains high,
They seek the heavens, they touch the sky.

With every step upon this earth,
They find the weight of spirit's worth.
The echoes call in harmonies,
As nature sways, a heart's reprise.

For those who roam, both near and far,
Their journey marked by every star.
Each path they tread, a story told,
In vibrant colors, both meek and bold.

Where shadows linger, they find the light,
In every challenge, they take flight.
With voices raised in sacred song,
They celebrate where they belong.

So heed the tales of wanderers lost,
For in their journeys, wisdom's tossed.
Each praise song sung is a beacon bright,
Guiding the hearts toward the light.

Testaments Written in the Gravel

In the quiet earth, a whisper flows,
Hidden truths where the wild wind blows.
Each footprint tells a tale untold,
As faith like seeds finds ground to hold.

Beneath the skies, the stones align,
Chiseled by time, a sacred sign.
In every crack, the light shines through,
A reminder of paths we pursue.

The weary souls, they gather here,
With humble hearts, they cast aside fear.
For in each shadow, hope does rise,
Testaments breathed beneath the skies.

Hands of the faithful carve their dream,
In silent echoes, love's soft gleam.
Each line a promise, a covenant strong,
In gravel's embrace, where we belong.

So tread with grace on this sacred ground,
In gravel's testament, our faith is found.
Let every step be a prayer sincere,
In each silent moment, God's voice we hear.

The Untold Stories of Outcasts

Amidst the shadows, they walk alone,
With weary hearts, their struggles shown.
Forgotten whispers, a cry in the night,
In the arms of grace, they find the light.

Their stories woven in threads of pain,
Shunned by the world, yet hope remains.
Each life a canvas, each tear a hue,
Painting redemption in shades so true.

In every laughter, a hint of sorrow,
Yet still they rise to greet tomorrow.
Wounded souls seek a refuge divine,
A sheltering love, eternally mine.

For in each outcast, a spark of grace,
A holy flame in a desolate place.
They gather strength where others retreat,
In the heart of darkness, they stand on their feet.

So hear their voices, let them be free,
In untold stories, we all agree.
For every soul bears a light so bright,
In the depths of despair, hope takes flight.

Hymns for the Reluctant Traveler

On winding roads, the journey begins,
A hesitant heart where fear often wins.
With every step, the unknown calls,
In softest whispers, the Spirit enthralls.

Carrying burdens too heavy to bear,
Yet faith takes flight in the open air.
Each mile a lesson, each turn a chance,
To dance with grace in the divine's expanse.

Through valleys low and mountains high,
The reluctant traveler learns to fly.
With eyes wide open, the world unfolds,
Each hymn a story, a promise of gold.

In solitude's embrace, the heart finds peace,
With every heartbeat, doubts begin to cease.
A road less traveled, the Spirit leads,
With hymns of courage, the soul proceeds.

So wander forth, in faith let go,
For in the journey, true love will grow.
In every step, let your heart sing loud,
For the reluctant traveler, God is proud.

Blessings in the Brokenness

In shattered places, grace appears,
Fractured edges soften our fears.
Each crack reveals a story of old,
In brokenness, the heart turns bold.

For every wound, a blessing blooms,
In fields of sorrow, hope finds rooms.
Amid the ruins, love takes its stand,
A guiding light, a gentle hand.

With bowed heads, we gather near,
Each tear a testament, each sigh sincere.
In the depths of pain, we find our song,
In being whole, we'll learn to belong.

Through trials faced, the spirit grows,
In every sorrow, the blessing flows.
Embrace the cracks, let the light through,
For in brokenness, we find what's true.

So raise your voice, in unity sing,
For blessings unfold in the broken ring.
In finding beauty in every ache,
The heart awakens, no longer to break.

Ascending from the Ashen Ground

From ashes rise the spirits bright,
Hope ignites in darkest night.
With every tear, a seed is sown,
In hearts once shattered, love is grown.

The path ahead, through fire and flame,
Cleansed by trials, we call His name.
Faith's embers glow, through every test,
From ashen ground, we seek our rest.

In light's embrace, we find our way,
Each step with grace, we humbly pray.
The burdened soul, lifted high anew,
In sacred trust, we walk on through.

With every breath, we claim our prize,
A glimpse of truth beneath the skies.
In love's embrace, we are reborn,
From darkened nights, to golden morn.

Together we march, hand in hand,
With faith as our guide, we take a stand.
In unity's song, let hope resound,
Ascending forth from ashen ground.

In the Valley of Wayward Steps

In the valley where shadows creep,
With hearts unsteady, we search and weep.
A path uncertain, lost and blind,
Yet in the silence, the truth we find.

Echoes of doubt whisper in night,
Yet faith, a beacon, shines so bright.
Through wayward steps and trails of sorrow,
Hope leads us forth to a brighter morrow.

With every stumble, strength draws near,
In weakness found, His voice we hear.
Through valleys low, His hand we cling,
From brokenness, new life can spring.

In the embrace of the One who saves,
We dance on paths through liquid waves.
The wayward heart learns to forgive,
In grace's arms, we truly live.

So tread we softly, with humble hearts,
Each step, a journey, each moment, art.
In the valley's depth, we bear the test,
For wayward souls shall find their rest.

The Promise at the Cleft

In the cleft of stone, whispers flow,
Where hidden light begins to grow.
A promise made in sacred trust,
In shadows cast, our spirits rust.

When storms arise and fears take hold,
In quiet strength, His truths unfold.
The cleft reveals a way to see,
Through trials fierce, we seek to be.

With humbled hearts, we seek to know,
The depths of love that He will show.
In every crack, a chance to heal,
The brokenness, a sacred seal.

The promise waits in sacred space,
With open arms, we seek His grace.
In the cleft of all that we endure,
We find a love forever pure.

So when the night feels dark and long,
Remember this truth: you are not wrong.
For in the cleft, His light will shine,
A promise given, your heart is mine.

Labyrinth of Faith and Fracture

In a labyrinth where shadows cling,
Faith beckons softly, a gentle spring.
Through walls of doubt and paths unkind,
In every turn, a truth we find.

Fractured souls, we wander lost,
Yet through the trials, we count the cost.
The winding paths, they twist and bend,
Lead us to grace, our wounds to mend.

With every step, a choice unfurls,
In faith's embrace, the spirit swirls.
Through tangled turns and darkened fears,
We find our strength through all the tears.

Yet shadows fade when hearts stand strong,
In unity's song, we all belong.
So navigate with faith, not sight,
For love will guide us through the night.

Within this maze, hope's echo calls,
In faith's embrace, we rise and fall.
The labyrinth holds our many scars,
But through the storm, we'll reach the stars.

Tribulations on the Sacred Trail

In shadows deep, we walk alone,
With heavy hearts, we seek the stone.
Through trials fierce, our spirits bend,
Yet faith, our guide, will never end.

The path is steep, the thorny ground,
Each step we take, our prayers abound.
With every tear, a story we weave,
In sacred trials, we learn to believe.

In whispers soft, the Spirit calls,
Through darkest nights, our spirit enthralls.
And in the fire, our souls are forged,
On sacred trails, our lives enlarged.

With weary feet, we rise and fight,
For in the storm, we find the light.
The trials faced, they shape our fate,
With love and grace, we navigate.

And as we walk, we leave our mark,
In every step, igniting spark.
For every tribulation faced,
Brings forth the joy, of hope embraced.

Rebuilding the Pilgrim's Way

Brick by brick, we mend the road,
With humble hearts, we share the load.
From ashes rise, our spirits soar,
In unity, we build once more.

The stones we lay, a gentle sigh,
Each act of love, a whispered cry.
From wounds of past, new life will bloom,
Together we chase away the gloom.

With faithful hands, we clear the path,
In every smile, we count the math.
The journey far, yet close in grace,
In sacred spaces, we find our place.

We gather strength from broken dreams,
And reshape life with hopeful themes.
The pilgrim's way becomes our guide,
With every step, arms open wide.

For in each heart, the truth resides,
In every soul, the spirit guides.
Together we rise, renewed, restored,
In love's embrace, we are adored.

The Stones Cry Out in Silence

In quietude, the stones repose,
Whispers hidden, the truth bestows.
They bear the weight of sacred tales,
In silent grace, the spirit sails.

With every crack, a voice resounds,
Echoing love, in holy bounds.
The past we carry, the stories vast,
In stones, the echoes of the past.

They witnessed tears, the laughter bright,
Through darkest days, they hold the light.
Each grain of sand, a promise made,
In sacred silence, the truth conveyed.

With every quake, the call arises,
In stillness found, our heart specializes.
Though silent, they cry out in love,
A dance of faith, a gift from above.

So let us listen, with hearts unveiled,
In quiet stones, the truth is hailed.
For in their depths, a song we find,
The stones cry out, our spirits aligned.

Signs of Hope Along the Wounded Path

In weary steps, the path unfolds,
With every trial, a tale retold.
Through brokenness, we search for light,
In shadows cast, we find our sight.

The signs of hope, like stars they gleam,
A gentle reminder, to dream the dream.
In every heart, a flame ignites,
Guiding us through the darkest nights.

With every wound, a lesson learned,
In every setback, our spirits turned.
The wounded path embraces all,
With tender love, we rise, we fall.

In beauty found, amidst the pain,
The sign of hope, like gentle rain.
For every struggle, the grace bestowed,
In love's warm embrace, we are consoled.

As we journey on, let faith remain,
In every heart, a refrain.
For signs of hope will lead us through,
On wounded paths, we are made new.

The Silent Echoes of Forgotten Blessings

In shadows cast by ancient trees,
Whispers of love from the skies tease.
Each leaf a prayer, softly speaks,
A touch of grace our heart still seeks.

The rivers hum a sacred tune,
Beneath the gaze of the silver moon.
Memories linger, though times may fade,
Within our souls, their warmth is laid.

In the silence, blessings unfold,
Stories of old, in silence told.
Each moment bears the weight of grace,
In humble hearts, we find our place.

The dawn breaks forth with gentle light,
Painting hopes on the canvas of night.
With every heartbeat, we are blessed,
In the quiet, our souls find rest.

Echos of love, a sacred bond,
In every challenge, we respond.
With open arms, we embrace the call,
For in forgotten blessings, we stand tall.

A Lament on the Winding Journey

Through valleys deep and mountains high,
We traverse the paths, with hearts that sigh.
Each step a burden, a story to tell,
Of trials endured and battles fell.

Oft lost in shadows, we search for light,
In the tapestry of day and night.
The winds of change whisper our plight,
Guiding our hearts towards the right.

Yet in the distance, hope shines bright,
A glimmering star in the darkest night.
With each lament, strength we find,
In the journey's pain, the soul's design.

With weary feet, we walk this road,
Laden with promises, our heavy load.
Yet in each sorrow, a lesson blooms,
Out of the dark, the spirit consumes.

Through winding paths, we learn to trust,
In faith's embrace, we rise from dust.
For every lament, there lies a song,
In the journey's heart, where we belong.

The Spirit's Dance on Weathered Ways

On cobbled stones where shadows play,
The spirit twirls in a bright ballet.
With every step, the past revives,
In every turn, the soul still strives.

Beneath the sky, both vast and blue,
The dance of light in morning dew.
Each breath a rhythm, a sacred beat,
In the dance of life, we find our seat.

In every sorrow, we find our grace,
As the spirit moves, we embrace the space.
With laughter ringing, joy shall flow,
In the dance of the heart, we always grow.

Through the darkened woods and fields of gold,
The spirit's tale will ever be told.
With hands held high and voices raised,
In life's great dance, we are amazed.

The weathered ways may wear us thin,
Yet in the dance, we always win.
For through each pirouette, we shall find,
The spirit's grace, our souls entwined.

Learning to Walk in the Wilderness

In the tangled brush where silence grows,
We seek the path that wisdom knows.
With every footfall, lessons rise,
In nature's arms, the spirit flies.

Wilderness whispers, both soft and loud,
In moments of doubt, we stand unbowed.
The echoes of truth, a guiding song,
In the heart of the wild, we belong.

We stumble and fall, yet rise in grace,
Learning to journey, we find our place.
With eyes wide open, the world reveals,
The beauty in wounds and the strength that heals.

Through brambles thick and streams so clear,
We shed our burdens, we cast out fear.
Each step a story, a truth to share,
In the wilderness wide, we learn to care.

With every sunrise, hope ignites,
In the heart of the wild, the spirit fights.
Through learning and love, we walk as one,
In the wilderness learned, our journey's begun.

Among the Ruins

Amidst the stones of yesterday,
Whispers of grace can be found,
Lost souls seek in devastation,
The sacred voice that resounds.

In shadows deep, the heavens cry,
Echoes of brokenness weave,
Yet in despair, a hope does lie,
For it's in the silence we believe.

Dust and ashes speak of strife,
Yet faith ignites a flame,
Through the cracks of a weary life,
God's light calls us by name.

Hands raised high, we reach for sky,
From the ruins, we shall rise,
In every tear, a battle cry,
For love is stronger than our sighs.

So tread we now on battle ground,
In unity with spirits bold,
Among the ruins, grace is found,
In stories of the brave retold.

Hope Shall Rise

In the dawn of each new day,
Hope arises from the mire,
With every prayer we humbly say,
Strength is born from our desire.

Through storms that rage and winds that wail,
A beacon shines through darkest night,
On paths where shadows weave a tale,
The heart remembers what is right.

In valleys low and mountains high,
Hope whispers softly in the breeze,
Unseen, yet ever drawing nigh,
A gentle touch that brings us peace.

Time may steal our fleeting breath,
Yet never can it steal our faith,
For even in the face of death,
Love's promise grants a boundless wraith.

So with each step, we rise anew,
In every heart, a sacred flame,
Hope shall rise, forever true,
To sing the world a brighter name.

Pilgrimages of the Heart

Every journey finds its start,
In whispers deep, a sacred call,
With open hands and humble heart,
We answer love's resounding thrall.

Across the lands, our spirits roam,
Seeking truth in every face,
The path we walk, we call it home,
And grace is found in every place.

Through trials faced and burdens borne,
Our faith like stars will guide the way,
In every tear, a promise worn,
That light shall break the gloom of day.

With raptured souls, we find our grace,
In kindness shared along the road,
Each step we take, a slow embrace,
The weight of love our heavy load.

So let us wander, hand in hand,
For every heart is worth the quest,
In pilgrimage, together stand,
In love, we find our truest rest.

Rebirth from Dust and Shadows

From ashes born, we rise and soar,
In shadows long, we find the light,
In every ending, there's a door,
To new beginnings, pure and bright.

Life's trials may shape the weary soul,
Yet spirits soar on wings of grace,
In every crack, we find the whole,
Rebirth ignites our sacred space.

In every heart, a story weaves,
A tapestry of hope and pain,
For every loss, the soul believes,
In love we find the strength to gain.

So let us dance upon the dust,
With joyful hearts that leap and shout,
For every moment brings its trust,
In life's great circle, we find out.

From shadows deep, we rise anew,
Embracing light with open arms,
In every heartbeat, love shines through,
Rebirth from dust, in spirit charms.

Chasing Light in the Chasm

Through the chasm, dark and wide,
We bravely seek the shining ray,
For hope is born when faith's the guide,
In every step upon the way.

With hearts ablaze, we crave the day,
Where shadows flee from morning's kiss,
In every tear, we pave our way,
With courage found in love's sweet bliss.

For darkness, though it looms so near,
Cannot extinguish truth's warm flame,
In every doubt, we face our fear,
And rise again, a new acclaim.

So chase the light with fierce intent,
From chasms deep, we shall emerge,
For where our souls and hearts are bent,
Love's light will always be the surge.

In whispers soft, the promise calls,
That light shall break the deepest night,
In unity, our spirit thralls,
Chasing light, we find our might.

Redemption Awaits Along Worn Trails

In the quiet shadows of the trees,
Hope whispers softly in the breeze.
Each step we take, a prayer unspoken,
Hearts reborn where vows are broken.

Paths once lost now gently lead,
To sacred grounds where souls are freed.
Through rugged ways, our burdens shared,
The light of grace has always cared.

In weary hearts, a flicker bright,
Guides us home through darkest night.
With every stumble, hands that lift,
Redemption waits; it's Heaven's gift.

Worn trails bear witness to the past,
Yet love sustains, our shadows cast.
In patience strong, we find the key,
To the promise of eternity.

So tread with trust, the road ahead,
With faith, our spirits gently fed.
For what is lost can still be found,
In God's embrace, we are unbound.

Signs of the Wayward Flock

In fields of doubt where shadows creep,
We wander far, our hearts to keep.
Yet signs appear to guide our way,
Like stars that shine in night's array.

Each wayward step, a lesson learned,
In trials faced, our spirits burned.
A shepherd's call, so soft and near,
In every loss, He draws us near.

With gentle hands, He points the path,
Away from pain, away from wrath.
The flock may stray, yet never fear,
For love remains forever near.

Echoes of faith in voices blend,
Together we rise; together we mend.
In unity, our strength is found,
In faith's embrace, we are unbound.

So heed the signs along the way,
For love will lead at break of day.
The wayward flock shall find their rest,
In the Savior's arms, forever blessed.

Mending Souls on Winding Streets

On winding streets where shadows play,
We seek the light to guide our way.
Broken hearts find solace here,
In gentle hands that tend, not fear.

Each corner turned reveals the grace,
Of love unearned, a warm embrace.
With every tear, there springs a song,
To lead us where we all belong.

In friendships forged through trials faced,
We come together, lives embraced.
On crooked paths, we bend and bow,
And learn to trust in love, and now.

The streets may twist, yet hope endures,
A promise kept that love assures.
With every soul that finds a friend,
We mend the world, where hearts can blend.

So walk with grace on every street,
For every stranger, hope we meet.
In unity, our journey leads,
Mending souls, fulfilling needs.

Faith in the Fissures

In cracks of stone where light breaks through,
A flicker of hope, a promise new.
When darkness clouds the weary mind,
In faith's embrace, a truth we find.

Through shattered dreams and whispered fears,
Courage comes alive through tears.
In fissures deep, a seed is sown,
Restoring strength we thought was gone.

With every trial, our spirits soar,
From brokenness, we're made much more.
In tiny cracks, the light shall shine,
Reminding us of love divine.

So hold the faith through storms that rage,
For in the gaps, we turn the page.
As hearts align and hope ignites,
We dance with joy in sacred nights.

For faith sustains, though storms may wail,
In fissures wide, our truths prevail.
We rise again, in love's embrace,
In every crack, a glimpse of grace.

Through the Cauldron of Trials

In the heat of the struggle, we kneel,
Seeking strength in the darkness, we feel.
With faith as our armor, we rise,
Through the fire, our spirits will prize.

Every tear is a prayer sent above,
In the cauldron of trials, we learn love.
Each hardship a lesson, each scar a grace,
In the depths of despair, we find our place.

The path may be rugged, the storms may roar,
Yet hope lights the way, forevermore.
Carried by angels, we tread the line,
Through the cauldron of trials, our souls shine.

From ashes to glory, we shall emerge,
With an everlasting spirit, we surge.
In unity we gather, hearts interlace,
With courage renewed, we embrace His grace.

The cauldron, a forge, where spirits are made,
In trials, our faith is designed and laid.
Reborn in the struggle, adorned in light,
We walk hand in hand, through the night.

The Saints Within the Fractured Way

When shadows loom over the broken path,
The saints within whisper peace from their wrath.
They guide us along where the lost wander,
With love in their hearts, our troubles they ponder.

In whispers of grace, their wisdom flows,
Through fractured ways, their presence glows.
They teach us to dance in the face of despair,
And find the divine in the burden we bear.

With hands outstretched, they gather the lost,
Reminding our souls of the heavenly cost.
Each footstep they take, a promise to keep,
In the fractured way, our spirits shall leap.

Through valleys of silence, through mountains of woe,
The saints walk beside us, their light we will grow.
Their courage ignites our unwavering quest,
In the fractured way, we find our rest.

Together in faith, we'll carry the flame,
In the hearts of the saints, we rise without shame.
Through trials and triumphs, forever we stray,
Embracing the path of the fractured, the way.

The Morning Star Above the Ruins

Amidst the ruins where shadows reside,
The Morning Star shines; our hearts open wide.
With a promise of dawn, hope's sweet embrace,
Guiding our souls to a sacred place.

In the wreckage of dreams, where darkness fell,
The light of the star casts a radiant spell.
With whispers of mercy, it calls us near,
To rise once again, to persevere.

Each broken brick tells a tale of the past,
Yet the Morning Star whispers love to us vast.
With patience it shows us the beauty in pain,
And in every trial, there's much to gain.

From the ruins we build, a foundation of grace,
The Morning Star watches, a celestial face.
Through storms and through trials, we shall not fear,
For in our rebirth, the dawn draws near.

So let us unite, with spirits so bold,
Finding strength in the light that we hold.
With faith as our guide, we'll rise from the gloom,
The Morning Star shines, dispelling the doom.

Redemption Paths in the Night

In the silence of night, where shadows conspire,
Redemption paths lead us through trials of fire.
With every step taken, a burden released,\nIn the arms of
His mercy, our fears are ceased.

As darkness envelops, our spirits ignite,
In the whisper of hope, we find our true light.
Each stumble forgiven, each heart set free,
On the paths of redemption, our souls come to be.

With candles of faith lit in the depth of despair,
We journey together, lifted by prayer.
Each moment a chance, each breath a new start,
In the tapestry woven, love fills the heart.

So fear not the night, for dawn shall appear,
With the promise of grace, our vision is clear.
On redemption paths, we shall carry the fight,
Together we'll triumph, emerge from the night.

Through valleys of shadows, through trials we tread,
In the warmth of His love, we are fully led.
With courage unyielding, our spirits take flight,
On the journey of faith, we embrace the night.

The Spirit's Route to Wholeness

In silent dawn, the Spirit calls,
To wander paths where healing falls.
With every breath, the soul aligns,
In whispered prayers, the heart entwines.

Through trials steep, and shadows cast,
In faith we walk, our doubts surpassed.
The light within begins to rise,
Awakening grace, our spirit flies.

Beneath the weight of worldly cares,
The spirit sings through earnest prayers.
For wholeness waits in sacred trust,
In every tear, we find the dust.

With every step, a lesson learned,
Through love and loss, our hearts are turned.
In unity, we find our place,
The spirit's route, a path of grace.

Embracing all that life unfolds,
The story written, yet untold.
In every breath, we find our song,
The spirit's route where we belong.

Wandering Through Charred Memories

In ashes deep, the heart still yearns,
For whispered tales and lessons learned.
Through charred remains, I seek the light,
In darkness thick, I cling to sight.

Memories flicker like fading stars,
Each moment held, our inner scars.
Yet in the wreckage, hope will bloom,
A fragrant promise to dispel gloom.

With every breath, I sift through pain,
In wandering thoughts, I break the chain.
For in the ruins, life persists,
A spark of grace, in love we trust.

Through storms of doubt and raging fire,
The spirit's call ignites desire.
Reviving strength from sacred ground,
In memories lost, true peace is found.

Each step I take brings wisdom near,
In charred remains, I find my cheer.
For wandering hearts, though weary, roam,
In distant lands, they find their home.

Grace Amidst the Cracks

In fractured paths, our spirits meet,
Through cracks of doubt, we find our feet.
For grace abounds where shadows linger,
Its gentle touch, a tender finger.

Through weary nights and troubled days,
In every trial, the heart displays,
The strength of faith in subtle ways,
A soothing balm for life's wicked maze.

From broken hearts, a chorus sings,
In shattered dreams, new hope takes wings.
Amidst the pain, compassion grows,
In love's embrace, the spirit knows.

Beneath the weight of worldly strife,
In every crack, there springs new life.
For grace does weave through seams once torn,
A tapestry of love reborn.

In silence deep, the spirit prays,
Through cracks of life, its light displays.
In every wound, a lesson speaks,
Grace shines forth where the spirit seeks.

The Light that Dims the Shadows

In twilight's glow, the shadows flee,
As light descends, we start to see.
Each glimmer bright, a guiding star,
In darkest nights, it leads us far.

Through every trial, the light persists,
A beacon bright, through misty mists.
In whispered truths, our hearts confess,
In light we find our souls' redress.

With every dawn, a chance to rise,
To shed the pain and clear the skies.
For light within ignites the flame,
To chase the shadows, none to blame.

Together, we walk the narrow path,
In light we learn to face the wrath.
For every shadow, a lesson shows,
The strength that comes from love that grows.

In love, the light will dim the fears,
As tears transform into bright cheers.
For in this light, we find our song,
The light that guides us all along.

Grace in the Gaps

In silence where shadows softly creep,
Divine whispers cradle, secrets to keep.
Between each moment, grace lingers near,
Filling the void, casting out fear.

When storms of life rage, hearts feel the strain,
In the cracks of our pain, love flowers like rain.
Hope's gentle touch, a balm for the soul,
In gaps of despair, we find ourselves whole.

Each breath a blessing, each heartbeat a prayer,
In moments of weakness, He's always there.
With hands that uplift, with mercy that flows,
In grace we are held, where compassion bestows.

As twilight descends, and chaos unfolds,
In whispers of light, every story is told.
Through valleys of sorrow, His presence we seek,
In gaps of our journey, He makes us complete.

So let us embrace all the trials we face,
For in every struggle, we find His grace.
In the spaces between, where faith guides the heart,
There's beauty in gaps, where love plays its part.

Treading the Mire of the Heart

In the depths of the mire, where shadows conspire,
We wander in silence, our spirits grow tired.
Yet hope is a lantern, flickering bright,
Guiding our steps, dispelling the night.

With each heavy footfall, we seek to pause,
Reflecting on love, the eternal cause.
Through tempests of sorrow, through valleys of sin,
A whisper of grace beckons us within.

Yet treading this mire is not done in vain,
For every step heavy is kissed by the rain.
In the struggle of hearts, we find our true song,
In the mire of life, we learn to belong.

As we lift our eyes to the heavens above,
Each tear that we shed, a gift wrapped in love.
From the depths of despair, we'll rise once again,
Treading the mire, our souls will not bend.

So let us embrace the journey we trod,
For in every heartache, we meet with our God.
In the mire we dance, hand in hand, side by side,
With faith as our guide, we'll never divide.

The Hidden Miracles in Fissures

In the cracks of our lives, where light dares to play,
There lies a miracle, hidden away.
In troubled waters, when hope feels so thin,
A glimmer of grace whispers, 'You can begin.'

Amongst the fractures, where hearts once broke,
Resilience blooms gently with every hope spoke.
In the fissures of time, and the pain we impart,
Miracles linger, stitching the heart.

With every shadow that darkens our way,
There's beauty unspoken, in dawn's bright display.
Through trials we wander, yet find strength anew,
Fissures hold treasures that lead us to true.

In prayerful reflection, with eyes set to see,
Each struggle transforms us, sets our spirits free.
For in every shard, a story unfolds,
Of healing and courage, more precious than gold.

So let us embrace, each crack that we bear,
For in hidden miracles, God's presence is there.
With faith as our anchor, we journey ahead,
In the fissures of life, His promise is spread.

Dust to Ashes

From dust we arise, to the heavens we soar,
Each breath a reminder, of what came before.
In the cycle of life, where endings meet grace,
We find our true essence, in the depths of His space.

For ashes may whisper of battles long past,
Yet hope born from struggle, is forever steadfast.
What crumbles to dust can be molded anew,
In the hands of the Maker, all things can renew.

The weight of the world may press down on our soul,
Yet within the fragility, lies the strength to be whole.
Through trials and tribulations, we learn to arise,
From dust to ashes, we begin to realize.

Each moment a canvas, painted with tears,
Through sorrow and joy, we conquer our fears.
So let us embrace wherever we fall,
From ashes to dust, we're held by His call.

For life is a dance, a rhythm divine,
In dust and in ashes, His love intertwines.
With every heartbeat, in grace we reclaim,
From dust into glory, we rise in His name.

Grace Renewed

In dawn's first light, a promise is born,
A whisper of mercy, a heart gently worn.
In each new beginning, grace weaves a thread,
Renewing our spirits, where hope is not dead.

Through trials endured, and sorrows embraced,
We gather our courage, in love we find grace.
When shadows surround us, with burdens we bear,
In the silence, He whispers, "I'm always there."

For every ending is but a new start,
With grace as our beacon, illuminating the heart.
In the dance of forgiveness, we learn to let go,
With eyes set on future, our faith starts to grow.

So let us rejoice in each moment we find,
The beauty of grace, in the ties that bind.
Through laughter and tears, His love will not fade,
In grace we are comforted, in grace we are made.

As seasons will shift, and life flows like streams,
We anchor in hope, like the stars in our dreams.
For in every heartbeat, and each breath we renew,
We walk in His grace, forever made new.

Milton Keynes UK
Ingram Content Group UK Ltd.
UKHW020041271124
451585UK00012B/986